John Lowe

A Lowe Publication™

Text © John Lowe, 2011.

The right of John Lowe to be identified as author of this work has been asserted by him in accordance with the Copyright, Designs and Patents Act 1988.

All rights reserved. No part of this publication may be reproduced or transmitted in any form or by any means, electronic or mechanical, including photocopy, recording or any information storage and retrieval system, without permission in writing from the publisher.

Published in 2011 by:

**Lowe Publications
Linen Hall, 162 Regent Street
London, W1B 5TG
United Kingdom**

ISBN: 978-1-907824-11-1

Layout and illustrations by Giorgio Giussani.

Edited by Judi Hunter.

Printed in London by Empress Litho Ltd.

Surviving redundancy is more about your attitude and skills and not about recessions and company closures. Surviving redundancy will make you more resilient to global downturns and less fearful of negative trends.

Contents

About the author	8
Surviving redundancy	10
Your personality profile	14
The Supporter	15
The Influencer	18
The Creative	21
The Analyst	24
The Supporter and redundancy	28
The Influencer and redundancy	30
The Creative and redundancy	32
The Analyst and redundancy	34
The job journey and age	36
Age and experience	36
Age and attitude	37
Changes in the employment market	38
Building your job profile	42
Personal preferences	44
Personal circumstances	49

Personal skills and experience	50
Remuneration	53
Your Job Profiler – an example	**58**
Conclusion	**60**

About the author

John Lowe, founding director of Regent Selection, Regent Coaching and Regent eLearning, is the author of *Your Lowe Profile* and one of the leading experts on career and personal development coaching.

John is a successful headhunter, recruitment consultant and coach and it is this rare combination of skills and his experience of having conducted over 20,000 interviews – all factors which collectively give him unique market and people insight. He personally coaches MBA students, university professors, Board directors and an extensive range of business executives.

The coaching always has a strong employability focus and John's first-hand knowledge of the market place is based on his expertise of conducting assignments with the world's largest corporations, SMEs and start-ups. Each industry and employment activity has its own dynamic and the structure and content of the coaching has been designed to embrace this divergence and variety. John has introduced an exciting new approach to conventional coaching through the identification and development of four distinct personality types. As the candidate recognises their type and individual strengths, they can then apply this knowledge to the critical employment stages of knowing what is their ideal job role, always successfully performing on interview and consistently enhancing a top performance at work. All these critical factors are described in the publication *Your Lowe Profile,* which can be used as an expert career coaching reference.

On a personal note, John is a graduate of the University of London where his Masters in Philosophy had a particularly contemporary focus on the role of ethics in our changing workplace.

This booklet will change your perspective on redundancy. Follow the coaching advice and you will view redundancy as an opportunity for positive career reappraisal, an opportunity to know your personality and recognise your real strengths. If it happens again, you will see 'new opportunities' and not 'out of work'. An inspiring motivational read.

Surviving redundancy

The reality is that many more employees will experience redundancy at some stage in their working career in the current fluid job market. It does not have to be a monumental global catastrophe such as the credit crunch. It can be a local event where cheaper imported products have created competition that cannot be matched, making the organisation no longer sustainable.

Employer relocation or technical skills becoming redundant are frequent causes for employers having to 'let you go'. It may happen at a critical stage when your salary is supporting a family and a large mortgage and therefore, with such dependencies, unemployment can directly affect all family members. Taking the children to and from school and shopping during the day may be new experiences, but ones you would happily swap for that full-time role and an annual income.

The job market is pyramidal in relation to salary and expertise. As you grow in salary and experience, the opportunities become fewer. Graduates leaving universities will have many more opportunities than CEOs on a multimillion package.

Whatever your age or experience, the reactions will always be individual. Loss of status and purpose can lead to negativity and vulnerability or, to others, a 'happy release' and looking forward to a more exciting opportunity.

There is a very positive tendency in today's market for mature candidates to undertake consultancy roles. This gives them the opportunity to capitalise on their operational experience, which they can apply to managing new projects with similar commercial objectives within disparate organisations.

Redundancy will have very different implications to different employees. You may be working for a large employer, have accrued a very favourable redundancy package and look forward to the opportunity to put your name forward for voluntary redundancy. Perhaps you have worked for the organisation for too many years and this presents the ideal chance to fund an early retirement.

For the purposes of this booklet, *Surviving Redundancy,* is more focused on the scenario of involuntary redundancy, which has come about as a result of your role becoming obsolete, a company closure or relocation, bankruptcy or that commonly-used euphemism 'downsizing'. How you react to redundancy will no doubt be determined by the circumstance, but more importantly it will be dependent on your personality type. Certain types will be pragmatic – 'That's life; it was inevitable' – and they will immediately consult the job boards and commence the process of job searching. Other types will take the bad news very personally and will require lots of encouragement to compensate for that low self-esteem tendency.

With the importance of personality in mind, I have described the main personality types and how each type reacts to the challenge of gaining re-employment.

You will find the paragraph on career skills to match the job advertisement particularly relevant. I regularly write advertisements for the worldwide job boards outlining the dominant skills required for the role. It is important, then, that you can identify your dominant strengths when you are searching the vacancies for that ideal match. In the meantime, the best way to survive redundancy is to get back into the job market. Knowing yourself better in terms of your real skills and then knowing how to apply this knowledge to the job market is the best starting point.

Your personality profile

Before you start rushing into investigating careers, it is a good starting point to recognise your own personality profile and your own skills. This section will introduce you to various personality profiles, which allow you to identify your personality characteristics to enable you to make better decisions about your career path.

My experience of interviewing and coaching has identified four personality types:

- **The Supporter.**
- **The Influencer.**
- **The Creative.**
- **The Analyst.**

We all have these traits in different measures.

To help you to identify your dominant personality profile, I have described the psychological characteristics of each type. Most people's behaviour will be influenced by two personality types: a dominant one and a secondary one. Identify your particular type. It will help you to understand your skills and capitalise on your positive strengths within a work environment. It will help you to understand why, historically, you did not enjoy certain work tasks and, conversely, why you were so successful in fulfilling certain roles.

The Supporter

In common parlance, the Supporter could be described as a 'people person'. They are good judges of character and have a strong ability to empathise with others. In terms of the corporate environment, the Supporter likes to display the following characteristics:

- Enjoys helping people and gaining recognition for doing so.
- Engages with colleagues on a meaningful and personal basis.
- Will support weaker members of a team and help them to develop.
- Empathetic and sensitive to others – strong aptitude for customer care and client services.

- **Dislikes confrontation and does not voluntarily interact with truculent, domineering types.**
- **A tendency to be over concerned regarding the sensitivities of colleagues and to lose focus in terms of commercial objectives.**

The strong people aspect of their personality will mean that their judgements and comments will be from the people perspective. Their descriptions will focus on the players rather than the game, the actors rather than the film, the personnel rather than the project.

Supporter – career skills to match the job advertisement

The Supporter is highly adaptable and can relate well to colleagues and technologies. When you are endeavouring to search job advertisements, you may find you have a wide choice. To refine your choice, follow these recommendations. The people contact should be in the context of training, helping, instructing or leading. Avoid roles that involve overt selling skills – this is ideally the Influencer's domain.

Whilst the duties and responsibilities of a role are important to all of us, you will find that a friendly collaborative working atmosphere will be most motivational. You will benefit from the team environment and perform better within this structure. Avoid roles that are isolationist and do not require people engagement. Doctors, nurses, lawyers and accountants can be Supporters and the majority of functional roles in most organisations will have Supporters as the most popular personality characteristic. So your choice is comprehensive.

Your major challenge will be following my advice above regarding the atmosphere criteria. To find out how well you might fit into the team, you can only really decide after your interview or when you have worked in the environment for some weeks. Do, therefore, pay particular attention to the detail of the advertisement and, whilst on interview, ask searching questions in terms of the people interaction aspect of the role. Look for advertisements that emphasise these skills: good communicator; team player; flexible; reliable; trainer; instructor; etc.

The Influencer

The Influencer is articulate and outgoing and may be described as being 'a good talker'. They are likely to display the following qualities:

- Outgoing and talkative.
- Enjoys the social aspect of the work environment. Has a wide circle of friends and dislikes 'sitting in'.
- A good leader whom others find inspirational.
- A strong negotiator and sales person.
- Likely to dominate group meetings.
- Highly political in a work environment.

An Influencer has good commercial acumen and can be motivated with the prospect of earning commission or a bonus based on performance. They will endeavour to take up promotion opportunities and, consequently, can move up the career ladder faster. A higher income also gives them the option to indulge in 'good taste' for expensive purchases.

Influencer – career skills to match the job advertisement

Look for a role with a high level of people interaction whereby you have the opportunity to persuade, sell and influence. There should be scope to earn fees or bonuses based on your own success. The product or service you are promoting should not be too technical, as you will only be happy presenting the 'big picture' rather than the minutiae. The selling cycle should not be too protracted. Long-term negotiations normally involve complicated product or service specification and will not offer a productive platform for the Influencer to apply their strong persuasive skills. You will be capable of selling on a one-to-one basis, to groups and to senior Boards. The greater the audience, the more you will rise to the challenge. You enjoy variety in terms of dealing with different clients and also in terms of location. You should not just be office bound.

Look for jobs with the following components:

- People contact – to persuade, to influence.
- Service/product – not too technical – which can be effectively introduced and described via a presentation or on an individual basis.
- Variety – different clients, different location.
- Financial reward based on performance.

Pay particular attention to advertisements where the following skills are highlighted: strong communicator, results orientated, commission/bonus paid on results, target driven, challenging, motivator, decisive.

The Creative

The Creative is a lateral Analyst with the ability to think 'outside the square' and bring a fresh, original perspective to workplace challenges. The following characteristics are typical of the Creative:

- A creative aptitude, which can manifest as a special design talent or a strong appreciation of the arts.
- Takes nothing for granted.
- Enjoys new ideas and non-traditional routes to problem solving.
- Confidently states opinions on advertising campaigns, market trends and future product and lifestyle developments.
- Over sensitive at times and does not take criticism well.
- Has difficulties with time management and works on the philosophy of 'Give me more time and I can do an even better job.'
- Has 3D visualisation.

Creative – career skills to match the job advertisement

The Creative should seek only roles where there is scope to apply their talent. This can be in many forms. You may be designing, composing, writing, painting, commissioning or briefing designers, studio managing or you may be project managing the creative processes ensuring brand integrity and brief compliance. You may seek roles to apply your own creative specialism or, as a manager, to brief the creative team.

You may enjoy manifesting your creative skills in the field of literature, music or the fine arts, or you may apply your unique talent to the more functional attributes of daily life. Design skills are latent or overt in all products we use – cars, furniture, houses, interiors, offices, mobiles, computers and packaging. Creativity is a unique skill and whatever your experience and seniority, whether you are seeking a junior, middleweight or director level role, you should always ensure that there is a design or creative component compatible with your ideal career aspiration and talent. Otherwise, you will feel frustrated and bored and compelled to seek a new opportunity.

The work should have strong, challenging and varied components. Creatives tend to change jobs more than average. Creative design assignments have definitive time spans and 'treading water' or waiting for the next challenge is not the Creative's normal or comfortable remit. Hence, working freelance on an assignment-by-assignment basis can suit well in terms of optimum application of skills.

When you are job hunting, you must decide whether you are seeking a role to demonstrate and apply your particular skills or whether you are seeking a role whereby you are facilitating third-party ideas and recommendations.

Look for advertisements describing the role as challenging, requiring a strong creative/design component and a positive proactive mentality. Look for roles with new unique challenges that do not contain repetitive boring elements.

The Analyst

The prevailing quality of the Analyst is the ability to approach and solve problems in a highly rational, structured manner. In terms of personality characteristics, the following are likely to apply:

- Enjoys the challenge of working things out independently.
- Enjoys problem solving – the greater the problem, the greater the challenge and the greater the intellectual satisfaction.
- Happier expressing facts over feelings.
- Lacks motivation if the task in hand is perceived to be pointless.
- Enjoys their own company.
- A good listener.
- Lacking in verbal spontaneity.

The Analyst is clinical in their judgements. They are not predominately people oriented and have a clear focus on the task in hand. The Analyst can be considered introverted. They are thoughtful in response, rarely circumlocutory and only comment on what they know.

Analyst – career skills to match the job advertisement

The work environment is daily becoming more process-driven, whereby technology takes over the role of people. This development means there will be a growth in technology-related roles and it is important that you keep up to date with new emerging processes. You should continually look for courses or roles that will not just match but positively challenge and enhance your skills.

The dominant role of the Analyst is to offer a specialist technical skill to their employer, whereby soft skills are a secondary consideration. Your expertise is in what you know and your ability to apply your knowledge. A heart surgeon, a mathematical modeller, a jumbo jet pilot and a software engineer are employed predominantly for their technical expertise, and not for their amazingly friendly disposition or tacitness, these behaviours are less consequential. Clinically, scan the job boards for roles capitalising on your technical abilities. You should avoid roles with a high content of people dependent interaction such as sales or training. Analysts do not enjoy pressure selling and do not have the patience to be successful instructors. When the role has a people persuasive element or your work is supportive of sales presentations, you will have to be careful that you are not drawn into a sales type role that will not suit your personality. A salary where a large component is bonus or commission may be an indication that there is an obligation to perform and achieve, i.e. to sell. Avoid these advertisements.

The Analyst enjoys getting involved in technical work. You should therefore search for roles that will capitalise on your aptitude for engaging with complicated data, technical or scientific-based issues. The Analyst has strong management skills where projects involve a high degree of analysis and problem solving.

As an Analyst, you may have a tendency to understate your abilities and be over cautious in the roles for which you apply. Remember, new technologies are new to all candidates and you will have the aptitude and propensity to absorb new developments – be ambitious in your applications.

The Supporter and redundancy

The Supporter is always sensitive to dramatic changes and can develop an attitude of low self-esteem when they are made redundant. They will have a tendency to take the experience very personally and, though there is no real fault factor, they can irrationally blame themselves for situations beyond their control. They will over exaggerate the negative aspects and worry about the financial implications of having no income:

How can I survive on no salary? The job market seems very slow and I have applied for jobs but have not yet had any interviews. It's three months now since I was made redundant. The longer this goes on, the worse it's going to get.

We must agree that this is a very human reaction. Understandably, the Supporter feels as though their life has been put on hold and, until they secure a new role, they will feel insecure. Supporters are very sociable with a wide circle of friends. The fact that they are unemployed will add additional pressure to the situation as it directly affects their relationships: no drinks after work; no work presents to buy or birthday cards to sign; and no politics to discuss.

The Supporter will benefit from a structured approach to job searching. This will help to compensate for the emotional reaction.

The Influencer and redundancy

The Influencer will not cope well with compulsory redundancy. Their negative reaction can be mitigated by the circumstances. If they feel that the circumstances are not a personal reflection of their performance or ability, i.e. it is beyond their control or influence, then this important factor will help to counter their tendency for developing a negative attitude.

The Influencer is very ego driven and, thus, will be very defensive of events that might 'doubt' that ego; they will indulge in vociferous explanations outlining how redundancy came about, making sure that the audience is fully aware of the factors beyond their control. 'Forty others were made redundant the same day,' and 'I believe in the last month they have let another 30 go. I don't think the company will last long.'

Similar to the Supporter, the Influencer must endeavour to focus on the challenge to gain a better and more exciting opportunity, thus reducing the emotional and highly personal element of redundancy. This positive action will help to counter the issue of vulnerability and the natural tendency to develop low self-esteem.

Influencers enjoy roles where they are rewarded and recognised for their achievements. The downside of this is that, if they do not achieve their targets, they may be dismissed on the grounds of lack of performance. This is a natural corollary when you choose roles with scope for high earnings based on high performances.

The Influencer is very sociable and will have a wide circle of friends. They talk openly about themselves and their job and can be boastful when expressing their work performance. Therefore, the loss of a job can be potentially stressful and the ensuing loss of status can demolish their credibility when they were always giving a very upbeat reaction in terms of their work achievements.

If you are an Influencer, you will benefit from the following sections that encourage you to take a structured approach to job hunting.

The Creative and redundancy

Similar to the Analyst, the Creative does not dwell only on the emotional aspects of redundancy. Fair or unfair, they can move on and commence the exercise of seeking alternative employment. The short-term nature of today's employment market suits the Creative's mentality and need for new challenges. Freelancing has become commonplace as a feature of design work in that it is most project-specific. This endemic feature of their work means that Creatives can adopt and adjust well to change, be it voluntary or involuntary.

The Creative is predominantly task rather than people focused. They do not indulge in office politics and will judge executive decisions in the commercial context. I have often interviewed candidates who were charged with the task of conducting a report on their department, which concluded with the recommendation that their role become redundant.

I am sure that the Supporter and Influencer would have extreme difficulty at arriving at such a conclusion. The

Creative is probably the best equipped attitudinally in the marketing of themselves after redundancy. Their philosophical objective approach, whereby they can depersonalise the experience, bodes well in today's task-focused market.

The Analyst and redundancy

The Analyst will also be philosophical when they are made redundant. Unlike the Supporter and Influencer, they will not interpret the event as a personal affront, but rather judge it in the context in which it happened. The Analyst will judge events without emotive spin and are usually accurate in their assessment of situations. Therefore, sympathy from colleagues is not necessarily useful as Analysts know their skills and do not react positively to verbal feather-bedding.

The exercise of trawling many job boards and conducting deep searches is the natural remit of the Analyst. Their analytical, scientific and structured approach matches the skills and aptitude that best exploit today's technologies.

They will, however, need to keep pressing the refresh button and not become too cynical or sceptical, particularly when they are presenting themselves at interview. Here, they will be compelled to perform out of type and give an upbeat, positive account of their skills. They do not want to be considered as technically very competent but conversationally too reclusive.

The job journey and age

Ageism is a very topical issue in the UK employment market. Due to the perceived prevalence of age discrimination, the UK government has created legislation whereby it is unlawful to discriminate against a person in the selection process or workplace on account of their age. Interviewers may not ask a candidate their age, though a candidate may volunteer the information if they wish. Many candidates, of course, inadvertently highlight discrimination by age: 'I am a young 45'; 'I am a fit 50 year old.' The assumption to these statements is that 45 is an old age and that you are normally unfit if you are 50 years old.

Age and experience

I prefer to substitute age for an experience indicator when I am reviewing CVs. If you are 45 years and attended university, then you will probably have 20 years of work experience. Age matters because the correlation is that you grow in experience, gain more expertise and acquire more responsibility that may culminate in a Directorship within a large multinational organisation. Here age matters; your experience is invaluable and critical to the efficient management of the organisation, and this culmination of life experiences and management skills means that your career has exponentially grown and developed through challenging opportunities and financial reward. But the job market is not always so accommodating to the more experienced, older candidate. Their technical skills may have become redundant. Your long-term employer may have relocated abroad and, as your skills were very company specific, opportunities for re-employment may be rare.

Age and attitude

People grow older and develop different attitudes. Some become cynical, cranky and defeatist, others become tolerant and open minded. Often, as you experience more situations and events, and you acquire more knowledge, you become more judgemental and more opinionated. You know that you don't like Roquefort cheese because you have tasted it; you don't like golf because you have played it; you have not learned to swim because immersing yourself in water does not appeal; you do love tennis and you play regularly; you go to the gym twice a week and enjoy keeping fit; you don't go to sporting events but enjoy watching them on television; you don't enjoy IT as you find it too complicated and always have to refer to colleagues for advice.; you do enjoy training and coaching and helping colleagues at the office; the list goes on…

The advantage of age is that you can instantly refine your choice, but success in today's employment market demands a flexible and adaptable attitude.

Changes in the employment market

Many more mature employees will experience a sudden discriminator – the employment market has suddenly gathered speed through the advent of globalisation. Forward planning has become obsolete and the focus is dealing with the 'new'. A manager of a retail bank would, historically, have a full-time PA and concern themselves with executive decisions. My current business bank manager camps out in a borrowed office, has no PA, types all of his own correspondence and must engage with the technology and its developments. Many managers who could not cope with this radical change volunteer for redundancy and find it difficult practically and emotionally to adjust or obtain another role – many opt for early retirement.

Radical change occurs most markedly with technology; often, one's skills can become quickly redundant as certain software supersedes the software with which you were familiar and competent. Within IT, for example, early programming languages such as Fortran and Cobol are rarely used these days; programming has incorporated more object-orientations and, with the growth of the internet, other languages such as Java have become more popular. Despite the fact that the technology has overtaken you, do not be dispirited.

Job choice is a journey and, so, if you are towards the latter half of your career, you must accept the fact that you are in for a bumpy ride. If your technical skills are redundant, your interview presentation must focus strongly on your potential for skills transference. If the traits and characteristics, such as a positive attitude, flexibility, having an adventurous nature and 'can do' mentality, are presented powerfully and articulately as your dominant soft skills, you will be offered new roles.

Consult *Your Lowe Profile* or the booklet *Interviews: My Worst Nightmare* in this series if you wish to gain instruction on this type of interview preparation.

Building your job profile

Having discussed the different reactions to redundancy, I will now set out a proactive course, beneficial to all personality types, that you can use to get yourself back into the job market. Building a job profile is a great way of regaining some composure and gaining some direction for your next career step.

Your work experiences, your personal circumstances, your personal preferences and your personal development are never static. They are continually evolving and changing and your career goals and aspirations must reflect this change and adaptation.

If, by using a structured method, you can confidently define your ideal job profile incorporating your core skills, then this knowledge will help you to be more creative in your job search. You will confidently identify roles where, through skills transference, you can make a strong positive application. From my experience, many candidates are too insular in their job search and application of skills. There can be a tendency to underestimate their abilities, for example, not to apply for a particular role within an oil company as they have no previous experience of the industry.

Yet, frequently, employers do not require industry experience as the skills required are not industry specific. The purpose of this exercise, which invites you to define and review all the facets of a job profile, is to give you a stronger focus in terms of the roles you can target in your job search. To build a job profile you should incorporate the following five important elements, which, from research based on my interviewing experience, are considered to be critical to career choice:

- Personal preferences.
- Personal circumstances.
- Personal skills.
- Personal experience.
- Remuneration.

Using these parameters, you can build your job profile and use it for job applications and as a reference for generating a professional CV. Review your choices and transfer your conclusion and comments to create Your Job Profiler. Be mindful that this exercise is a process, a road of discovery, not a sudden revelation. Let's look at the first signpost.

Personal preferences

We all have individual dos and don'ts. Our choices are personal; they are not right or wrong and do not require justification or qualification. Reviewing your preferences helps you to focus on roles that fit your profile and eliminate those that clash with your selection criteria. Most candidates will consider the following options on a 'must have', 'must avoid' or 'don't mind' basis.

Location

- Do you prefer a rural location where you can drive to work, or do you prefer to work in a large commercial conurbation?

Many people will choose to work and live in the same area. They feel part of and engage with their community. Others will travel out of the area to work and feel that they neither have the time nor the inclination to integrate with the community.

- **Do you want to work from home or work in the office?**

This will often depend on your personality type; the Influencer and Supporter will appreciate the interpersonal dimension of working in the office, whereas the task-orientated Analyst will prefer to work from home because people interaction is not their main priority – they can exclusively focus, without interruption, on the task in hand.

Hours

Employers will normally have a culture of nine to five, or long hours incorporating indefinite finishing times – which is your preference?

- *Work is my life – I love it!*
- *I am a member of a canoe club and I enjoy the twice weekly practice sessions.*

- *It is important that I spend quality time with my family during the week as well as at weekends. Work/life balance is my priority.*
- *I don't have time for hobbies – we are too busy at work.*

People/task environment

These comparisons will be familiar to you from when you were introduced to the various personality types. Follow the advice. If you are an Influencer or Supporter, your preference will be for roles that have a high level of people interaction. If you are an Analyst or Creative, the focus on the role content will be your choice. The job description will highlight the required skills and you can ascertain if they match your dominant personality traits.

Employer

The larger organisation will have good sports and social facilities and can offer a more structured career path. The smaller organisation can offer better scope for initiative, greater opportunity to feel part of a team and provides an environment whereby you can make an identifiable contribution.

- Do you prefer a large or small organisation?
- Do you prefer the work environment to be within central or local government, not for profit, a charity or a commercial organisation?
- Is it important for your employer to be nationally or internationally based? Do you prefer a large corporate environment or a small, more intimate working atmosphere?
- Do you prefer your employer to be a long-established organisation or a new start-up?
- Is ethical trading important to you in terms of product or service? Do you need to know your employer's sustainability policy if they have one?

Summary questions:

- What are your choice areas of work?
- How far in distance and time are you prepared to travel, and what are the costs?
- Do you prefer a role that allows you to work from home occasionally/frequently?
- Are you prepared to work weekends?
- What are your chosen hours of work?
- Are you prepared to be away from home on business – how often – how long?
- Are there extra curricular activities that you would sacrifice for work or would like to continue, for example, sport, hobbies, social groups or charity work?

Personal circumstances

This topic highlights situations that limit your choice when searching for suitable roles.

- You may dislike a certain mode of travel.
- You cannot cope with the rush-hour crush.
- You have a relative whom you need to care for.
- You were born in a particular area and do not want to move despite the scarcity of employment opportunities.
- You need a minimum salary of…

Work content and challenge may then be secondary considerations to salary level. It is important to be realistic and confront factors that will limit your search options. All candidates have individual and particular dos and don'ts, and you should not view these restrictions negatively. They are just particular to you.

Personal skills and experience

You will have already identified, and be familiar with, your personality strengths that are frequently referred to as soft skills within a job description and may include being flexible, creative, industrious, ambitious, able to multi-task, and cope under pressure, etc.

Your particular skills will match your preference for a predominantly people or task environment, which you have previously reviewed. However, soft skills cannot be considered on a standalone basis. Your skills are facilitators in the application of your other range of talents – your technical expertise. Though we can refer to soft skills and technical skills as separate, they are interdependent.

Technical skills are quantifiable and can be readily matched to advertisements as you scan the job boards. Technical skills will be obtained through education and work experience. The final parameter in building Your Job Profiler is to examine the extent and time over which you have acquired these skills.

When recruiting, the advertisements I write will frequently specify, 'You should have at least 5 years experience' or 'Ideally you will have 2 years experience' and salary levels will directly reflect the experience required.

This section on your job profile has been a prompt to encourage you to look more intently at your job opportunities and to apply a more selective mentality to the exercise.

Before you complete Your Job Profiler, try the exercise on the next page for practice purposes.

Practice:

Write a sentence highlighting your soft skills and your technical skills, for example:

Your job profile

Personal skills

I believe I have good communication skills and have given many internal presentations to groups of 20 staff. I frequently manage conference calls on highly technical IT issues and have recently completed my MBA, which I consider to be an endorsement of my ambition and determination towards self-development.

> **Personal experience**
>
> I believe my History degree indicates my ability to decipher literary commentary and my two years experience as an Editorial Consultant for a leading magazine demonstrates my ability to choose topical subjects and to understand and apply my publishing expertise of copy writing, print production, marketing and distribution.
>
> Technical skills: literacy, journalism, production, publishing, marketing and distribution.
>
> Experience: literary training 3 years, publishing experience 2 years.

Remuneration

By reading advertisements you will, through live research, get a good idea of salary ranges. Salaries are a personal subject and will be determined by your job priorities and domestic commitments. If job content and challenge are your most important criteria, then you will compromise on salary. There is no right or wrong. Some roles require a flexible attitude as the income initially may be below your expectation, but after six months or a year it may increase dramatically, subject to your performance. I have recently interviewed a financial analyst specialising in Mergers and Acquisitions who is prepared to accept a 50 per cent salary reduction. His current role demands that he works 15 hours per day and many weekends. Work/life balance is his motivation.

Location can be a major determinant regarding salaries. Inner-city roles will normally carry a higher salary than a country or suburban location. The compensation takes into account the travel inconvenience and cost, as well as supply and demand.

Salaries can only really be determined on a one-to-one basis. The determinants are many and diverse and, therefore, throughout your working life, will require an adaptable and flexible approach, particularly during recessions and credit crunches. For instance, oil, pharmaceutical, finance, IT and consultancy have a reputation generally of being better paid than hotel and catering, whilst advertising, PR and design can be company dependent.

Salary packages will vary from employer to employer in terms of benefits. The range of benefits may include: basic annual salary and a commission or bonus (individual or company performance related), pension, which may or may not require an employee contribution (contributory/non-contributory), annual paid holiday, gym membership, maternity/paternity pay, private medical insurance, life assurance, flexible working hours, and share option schemes.

When reviewing vacancies, calculate your minimum salary in terms of your financial commitments, incorporating special factors such as commuting costs and, if relevant, accommodation. Be transparent about your salary expectations and if it is not specified in the advert, ask for clarification of the salary range. 'Should I discuss salary on interview?' 'Should I leave it until the second interview?' 'Will I appear too pushy or mercenary if I mention salary – they might think I am only interested in the money?' My advice is yes, do ask for clarification – it is not construed as a weakness – quite the reverse. 'I understand the salary range is…,' 'I am seeking a minimum salary of…' are construed as non-aggressive formats to introduce the issue of remuneration. Headhunters will often play an important role in the negotiation of final terms.

Salary negotiation can provoke fascinating and diverse reaction. Some candidates will view a salary very personally: 'I am certainly not accepting that offer – it is far too low – I am worth a lot more.' This personal affront response will be the likely domain of the Supporter and the Influencer, whilst the Creative and the Analyst will be pragmatic and look elsewhere for the more competitive income.

The employment market has become more fluid, whereby employment on a temporary/contract basis has increased dramatically. More frequently, salary negotiation involves agreeing an hourly or daily rate. Where a technical skill is the dominant prerequisite for the role, there is a higher incidence of candidates working on a non-permanent basis. Examples are Creatives being employed as freelancers and IT specialists working on a contract basis.

View all salary negotiations on a supply/demand non-personal basis and you will most likely achieve a fair and realistic conclusion for both parties.

Your Job Profiler – an example

Personal preferences

Location ✓ Hours ✓ Employer ✓ Travel ✓

Location: city, hours: 8-10 per day, employer: ideally corporate multinational, travel: public transport, journey time: max 45 mins, cost: max £100 per month

Personal circumstances

Family ✓ Location ✓ Financial ✓

Family: married, 2 children, mother in care, location: cannot relocate, financial commitments: mortgage, children, school, carer, household

Soft skills

Soft skills ✓

I believe I have good communication skills and have given many internal presentations to groups of 20 staff. I frequently manage conference calls on highly technical IT issues and have recently completed my MBA which I consider to be an endorsement of my ambition and determination towards self-development.

Personal experience

Technical skills ✓ Experience ✓

I believe my history degree indicates my ability to decipher literary commentary and my two years experience as an editorial consultant for a leading magazine demonstrates my ability to choose topical subjects and to understand and apply my publishing expertise of copy writing, print production, marketing and distribution.

Remuneration

Min requirement ✓ Ideal salary ✓ Benefits ✓

Min 50k to cover monthly commitments (cannot go under); ideal 65k (10k more than current role); must have health insurance, pension fund and lifecover - profit share would be considered

Conclusion

The vast majority of candidates I have interviewed have commented that they have benefited from the redundancy experience. It may have made them more resilient and the exercise of finding another job has better prepared them for a similar event. It has given them a better work focus and a more detached, less vulnerable mentality, realising that today's market is too fluid and short-termist to rely on job longevity. It has made them more confident about their marketability and the tasks requiring the identification of their skills has been motivational, promoting that self-confidence and self-awareness. They feel less vulnerable and know that they have a method for job searching to apply if they are made redundant in the near future. In fact, many candidates have proactively applied this self-awareness and used it to change role for better career scope and/or increased income.

When you are made redundant you will experience many emotional reactions, depending on your own character and the circumstances, ranging from shock, anger, loss of confidence, vulnerability to fear. Equally, you will receive a wide range of well-intentioned advice, which may be relevant or contradictory.

I have structured this booklet to be directional and you-specific. I have based it on my daily interactions with the employment market. I have married my experience as a coach and my experience as a headhunter to ensure that surviving redundancy has not got a remedial focus, but rather empowers you not only to survive but to capitalise positively on the redundancy experience.